A Deacon
Prays

"This wonderful collection of short prayers and devotions is just what the busy deacon needs. It is a trove of wisdom, insight, and humility written in an elegant, clear style that captures the very essence of prayer. Greg Kandra has created here a small library of spiritual nourishment, and we offer a prayer of thanks for his work."

William T. Ditewig
Former executive director
Secretariat for the Diaconate, United States Conference of Catholic Bishops

"There will be times when we are broken and doubt, but keep this book close: Greg Kandra's prayers will strengthen you and remind you why God called you to be a deacon."

Deacon Ed Shoener
President of the Association of Catholic Mental Health Ministers
Compiler and editor of *Responding to Suicide: A Pastoral Handbook for Catholic Leaders* and *When a Loved One Dies by Suicide*

"Well done, Deacon Greg! This is truly a unique contribution for the spirituality of deacons. One can tell it's personal and wholly drawn from practical experience, which is the best kind of spirituality. I'm excited to share it with my deacons."

Most Rev. W. Shawn McKnight
Bishop of Jefferson City

"The prayers in this book will serve as spiritual food and water, guiding users to an encounter with the Holy Spirit, leading to minds and hearts renewed."

From the foreword by Most Rev. Frank J. Caggiano
Bishop of Bridgeport

"*A Deacon Prays* is a powerful encounter with the Lord! This timeless treasury of original prayers and devotions will inspire and equip deacons to joyfully fulfill their ministry in the Church. This book is a must-have resource that will enrich the deacon's prayer life and motivate him to serve faithfully."

Deacon Harold Burke-Sivers
Author of *Father Augustus Tolton*

A Deacon Prays

Prayers and Devotions for Liturgy and Life

Greg Kandra

Ave Maria Press AVE Notre Dame, Indiana

Scripture texts in this work are taken from the *New American Bible, revised edition* © 2010, 1991, 1986, 1970 Confraternity of Christian Doctrine, Washington, DC, and are used by permission of the copyright owner. All Rights Reserved. No part of the *New American Bible* may be reproduced in any form without permission in writing from the copyright owner.

© 2021 by Greg Kandra

All rights reserved. No part of this book may be used or reproduced in any manner whatsoever, except in the case of reprints in the context of reviews, without written permission from Ave Maria Press®, Inc., P.O. Box 428, Notre Dame, IN 46556, 1-800-282-1865.

Founded in 1865, Ave Maria Press is a ministry of the United States Province of Holy Cross.

www.avemariapress.com

Paperback: ISBN-13 978-1-64680-017-9

E-book: ISBN-13 978-1-64680-018-6

Cover image © Lost and Taken, border © Getty Images.

Cover and text design by Christopher D. Tobin.

Printed and bound in the United States of America.

Library of Congress Cataloging-in-Publication Data
Names: Kandra, Greg, author.
Title: A deacon prays : prayers and devotions for liturgy and life / Greg Kandra.
Description: Notre Dame, Indiana : Ave Maria Press, 2021. | Summary: "In this collection, Greg Kandra offers prayers for a deacon to strengthen his spiritual life and enhance his ministry"-- Provided by publisher.
Identifiers: LCCN 2020052787 (print) | LCCN 2020052788 (ebook) | ISBN 9781646800179 (paperback) | ISBN 9781646800186 (ebook)
Subjects: LCSH: Deacons--Prayers and devotions.
Classification: LCC BV680 .K34 2021 (print) | LCC BV680 (ebook) | DDC 242/.69--dc23
LC record available at https://lccn.loc.gov/2020052787
LC ebook record available at https://lccn.loc.gov/2020052788

*Dedicated to
Deacon James Hynes,
1958–2008,
whose greatest prayer was his life*

Contents

Foreword by Most Rev. Frank J. Caggiano xi

Introduction 1

I. Prayers for Daily Life 5

    To Begin My Day 7

    Prayer before Work 8

    Prayer before Assisting at Mass 9

    Prayer of Thanksgiving after Mass 10

    Prayer at Midday 11

    Grace before Meals 12

    Prayer in Times of Stress or Anxiety 13

    Prayer for Discernment 14

    Prayer at Day's End 15

    A Prayer for the Pope 16

    A Prayer for My Bishop 17

    A Prayer for My Pastor 18

    A Prayer for My Parish 20

    A Prayer for My Marriage 21

    A Prayer for My Family 22

    Prayer of Praise 23

Prayer of Thanksgiving 24

II. Prayers for Ministry 25

Prayer before Serving the Poor 27

Prayer before a Wake 29

Prayer before a Baptism 30

Prayer before Witnessing a Marriage 31

Prayer before Preparing a Homily 32

Prayer before Benediction 33

Prayer before Chanting the Exsultet 34

Prayer before Preaching 36

Prayer before Teaching 37

Prayer before Visiting the Sick 38

Prayer before Visiting One in Hospice Care 39

Prayer before a Parish Meeting 40

Prayer before RCIA Meetings 41

Prayer before Prison Ministry 42

Prayer for Police Chaplains 43

III. Diaconal Prayers 45

Prayer to St. Stephen 47

Prayer to St. Lawrence 48

Prayer to St. Francis 49

Prayer for Diaconal Vocations 50

Prayer for Priests 51

Prayer for Deacons and Priests Who Have Left Ministry 52

Prayer for Newly Ordained Deacons 53

Prayer for Single Deacons 55
Prayer for a Deacon Who Has Died 56

IV. Seasonal Prayers 57

Prayer during Advent 59
Prayer on Christmas Day 60
Prayer for the Christmas Season 61
Prayer for Epiphany 62
Prayer for Winter 63
Prayer on Ash Wednesday 64
Prayer during Lent 65
Prayer on Easter Sunday 66
Prayer for the Easter Season 67
Prayer on Pentecost 68
Prayer at the Beginning of Summer 69
Prayer for Late Summer 70
Prayer for Autumn 71
A Prayer for November 72

V. Prayers of Petition 73

Prayer for Peace 74
Prayer for Those Who Are Hungry 75
Prayer for the Homeless 76
Prayers for Those Who Have Left the Church 77
Prayer for Hurting Families 78
Prayer for Understanding among People 79
Prayer for the New Evangelization 80

Prayer for a Community in Crisis 81
A Prayer for Life 82
Prayer in a Time of Pandemic or Other Disaster 84

VI. Devotional Prayers 85
The Way of the Cross for Deacons 87
A Deacon's Rosary: The Mysteries of Light 124

Prayer Intentions and Notes 137

Foreword

No human life can be sustained for very long without access to food. Nor can a person survive if denied access to clean water. Such human staples are taken for granted in many parts of the world. Sadly, they remain in short supply for millions, whose lives hang in the balance. For them, the frailty of human life is a constant struggle that reminds each of us of our common responsibility to provide the daily needs of every human person.

In his marvelous book *A Deacon Prays*, Deacon Greg Kandra reminds us that the same need for nourishment governs our spiritual lives. As our human bodies need food and water to remain healthy and strong, so too does our spirit require food of a different type. Earthly food and water may nourish our bodies, but the gift of prayer nourishes our spirits. Such food allows us to enter into ever greater communion with our Lord and Savior, who is the eternal Source of every blessing and grace. Without such spiritual food, our hearts can easily grow cold, our spirits overwhelmed with the daily challenges we face while hope becomes a distant promise.

It is striking to consider that when asked by professional pollsters, adult American Catholics overwhelmingly identified their single greatest need as learning how to pray. Many feel a deep hunger to learn the power of silence, to marvel at the beauty around them, to open their hearts to the presence of God, and to rediscover joy in life. When asked further, these same believers were uncertain how best to pray, assuming that prayer is a discipline of great complexity and sophistication, open only to the educated or ordained. Nothing could be further from the truth.

In this powerful book, Deacon Kandra has provided us with a series of prayers, written in simple but elegant words, addressing every circumstance and vocational aspect of a Catholic deacon's life, so that its users can be spiritually fed. St. John Vianney once remarked to his brother priests that prayer is nothing else but union with God. If prayer is entering into communion with God—a dialogue where I speak to God and have the courage to remain in silence, listening to what God may say in return—these prayers are a powerful way to begin a sacred dialogue that will nourish every spiritual need.

St. Teresa of Ávila once observed that prayer is like heavenly rain that waters the garden of our soul. It is spiritual water without which our souls cannot thrive. The prayers in this book will serve as spiritual food and water, guiding its users to an encounter with the Holy

Spirit, leading to minds and hearts renewed. At times, prayer may seem a daunting challenge. However, Deacon Kandra reminds us that it is as simple as offering the words of a prayer with a humble heart. God, in his great goodness, will give us the rest.

In a world where daily life is often lived with frenetic activity, overwhelmed with noise and distractions, and within a world that is ever more divided, Deacon Kandra's book has come just in time. May its prayers lead deacons everywhere, and others of us fortunate to own this gem of book, to eat deeply of the spiritual food that will nourish within us the serenity, unity, and peace that Christ wishes to give us. The only requirement for us is to meet the Lord in prayer.

Most Rev. Frank J. Caggiano
Bishop of Bridgeport

Introduction

Lord, teach us to pray . . .
—Luke 11:1

Years ago, I met a man who had just started the deacon aspirancy program in his diocese. He was completing his first semester of formation, and I asked him how it was going.

"I love it," he told me enthusiastically. "But you know what's been really challenging?" He seemed almost embarrassed to bring it up, but then added, sheepishly, "Praying." "Praying?" I asked. He explained. "I've always been a guy who does things. I'm used to being busy, doing things, praying with my hands, you know? What I do is my way of praying. But I've had to learn how to pray another way." I think most deacons can understand exactly what he means.

The diaconate, by its very nature, is a ministry of doing. Deacons are rarely still. The deacon is the guy who teaches, preaches, arranges, carries, facilitates, sets up, and takes down. He's perpetually shuttling between the parish and his home, his home and his job. His days are packed with deadlines to meet, classes to prepare, sick people to visit, meetings to attend, questions to answer, phone calls to return, and homilies to write. A parishioner once put it this way: "You know what the deacon is? You're sort of like the priest's helper." Well, yeah. Sort of.

But our place, our role in the Church, is so much more than that. The deacon is, fundamentally, one who serves; he is configured at ordination to Christ the Servant, and so he serves in a particular way the People of God and, through that, God himself. At any parish, he is usually in the thick of things. So it is only natural that those men who like to keep busy—who don't like to have idle hands—are attracted to this vocation.

But there are so many moments in the deacon's life when the best way for him to use his hands, and to use them to serve, is simply to fold them in prayer. This book is for those moments.

Throughout this little book, you will find opportunities for prayer that I hope are particularly helpful to your diaconal vocation—such as a prayer before chanting the Exsultet or a Rosary composed especially for deacons. But there are also prayers in this book that can be used by other people for different circumstances and occasions. The possibilities and purposes for prayer, after all, are boundless. It is my intent that these short prayers can be useful to almost anyone seeking to pin down their hopes, aspirations, doubts, and joys—and then somehow put them into words. At the end of the book, you will find space for writing out prayer intentions and notes.

St. Philip Neri once wrote, "It is an old custom of the servants of God to have some little prayers ready and to be frequently darting them up to Heaven during the day, lifting their minds to God out of the mire of this world. He who adopts this plan will obtain great fruits with little pain." Maybe, just maybe, some of the words in this book can help today's "servants of God" out of the "mire of this world."

I also think this collection of prayers might be especially timely. In early 2020, when the world confronted the coronavirus pandemic and churches everywhere were shuttered and ministries more or less suspended, I heard from a number of deacons who, in the first days of the crisis, seemed at a loss. "How can we minister to people if we can't see them, visit them?" they asked. "What can we do?"

Some deacons started recording or live-streaming reflections; others did short videos of the Liturgy of the Hours and posted them on social media. Others started working the phones, trying to contact parishioners to at least say hello and let them know they were remembered. But one deacon asked in frustration, "Shouldn't we be doing more?"

My answer then is my answer now: Maybe we need to do less. Maybe we need to refocus our energies and just be. Maybe God is asking us to work less and contemplate more, to busy ourselves with prayer. It's easy to forget that despite what the world may think (or what our pastors may believe), we who have consecrated our lives to God are more than functionaries. I've often said this during retreats and at convocations: Being a deacon isn't just about what you do. It's about who you are. And who we are draws inspiration and strength from our devotion to the Lord we love and from our desire to serve him however we can, whenever we can. And that means, above all, striving to be men of prayer.

My hope, my prayer, is that this book will help make that easier, directing our hearts to the great work of evangelization and service that lies at the root of this beautiful vocation. Lest we forget: it is work that we literally hold in our hands.

Deacon Greg Kandra
April 25, 2020
Feast of St. Mark, Evangelist

I.

Prayers for Daily Life

Let's face it: every day has its hills and valleys—and at times we can do little more than just pray. The deacon marks his day with the Liturgy of the Hours—bookending it with Morning Prayer and Evening Prayer. But there are often other moments in life that feel as though they need their *own* set of psalms.

Very often, simply living the routine of daily life can be a kind of prayer itself, a canticle of bewilderment, anxiety, or hope. The writer Anne Lamott has famously written that she thinks the two most popular prayers are "Help, help, help!" and "Thank you, thank you, thank you!" Those pretty much sum up the human condition, don't they?

But there are some moments in life that cry out for more, moments that can lift our hearts or bring us to our knees. We all live them. We all survive them. We feel the need to turn to God and say, "Got a minute? I need to get something off my chest."

We all try to pray our way through these moments. For a deacon, these times are opportunities to remember the complicated, challenging two worlds in which we live—the secular and the sacred—and to seek God's help in bringing them together.

So, we pray. We pray for patience, for persistence, for resilience. We pray to make it through another day. We pray that we remain close to God and that he remains ever near to us.

To Begin My Day

Good morning, God of creation.
Thank you for creating one more day,
one more chance to serve, to inspire, to hope.
Help me to rise like the sun,
to bring light and warmth and possibility
to so many who experience only darkness and despair.
Gracious Father,
Fill my heart with humility and love,
so that I may never forget that
I have been shaped from dust
and that my service to you began not in triumph,
but lying on the ground, facing the earth,
praying for the saints to pray for me.
I pray to them again this morning
and pray to you with wonder and trust and joy.
Good God,
I am your pencil, your brush, your hands.
I am your servant.
Guide me in your ways
and use me as you will.
This day is yours, and so am I.
Amen.

Prayer before Work

My Lord God,
As I prepare for another day of work,
come and work beside me.
Guide my hand, focus my heart, direct my thoughts,
to continue your creation throughout the world.
May I always remember that I serve you and others
by the work I do.
Give me a patient and joyful heart
to praise you, even when I grow weary,
and to give thanks, even if I feel overburdened.
Help me to seek you in everything,
and to watch for opportunities to serve others.
May my words and my work always point to you.
I offer this prayer, as I offer all things,
through your Son, Jesus,
who worked beside a carpenter,
who walked among fishermen,
and whose own life's work
led to the salvation of the world.
Amen.

Prayer before Assisting at Mass

Lord,
As I prepare to serve at your altar,
to serve your priest and your people,
guide my thoughts and actions only toward you.
As I vest, I put on Christ, and the armor of my vocation.
The alb reminds me of Baptism,
the beginning of my life of faith.
Cleanse my heart this day and make me new!
The stole, borne on my shoulder and crossing my heart,
reminds me of the Cross you bore for me
and the love I bear for you.
The dalmatic, robe of charity,
clothes me in the charism of my calling.
Entering your holy sanctuary,
may I walk behind you in joy,
beside you in patience, before you in humility,
doing all for you and with you
so that I may assist at this Mass as if it were my first,
my last, my only one.
Amen.

Prayer of Thanksgiving after Mass

Generous God,
Thank you.
Thank you for the privilege of serving at your altar,
the gift of being only inches away from bread and wine
becoming the Body and Blood of Christ.
Thank you for the gift of bearing witness to your love.
May I never weary of being there for you,
and always stand ready to serve.
May I always count this as one of the blessings of my life,
an honor that humbles me and gives glory to you.
In serving at your altar, help me to also serve the poor,
the hungry, the lonely, and those forgotten.
May I take from this moment of wonder and gratitude
your grace to carry out your Gospel into the world,
bearing with me your light and your love.
Amen.

Prayer at Midday

Lord God,
At the middle of my day,
I pause to whisper a word of thanks.
Thank you for being by my side
and offering me reassurance and hope.
God of time, who lives beyond time,
help me to make the most of each day.
May I make every moment an offering,
and every act and word a kind of service,
for I am your servant, O Lord,
and my hands and heart belong to you.
I pray this, as I pray all things,
through your Son, Jesus Christ.
Amen.

Grace before Meals

Good and generous God,
Bless us and this meal before us.
Bless those who planted it, grew it, harvested it,
planned it, and prepared it.
Bless your servants who desire to serve others.
Bless our brothers and sisters who hunger—
and not only for food.
Bless those who hunger for friendship,
for fellowship, for dignity, for love.
I pray that you feed them as you feed us.
I give glory and thanksgiving to you,
good and generous God,
praying for the day we will all join you
at your heavenly table.
Amen.

Prayer in Times of Stress or Anxiety

O God of comfort and hope,
I need you now more than ever.
You have told us, "Be not afraid,"
but everything seems so uncertain.
There is so much that is unknown
and that causes me to be afraid.
Help me conquer fear.
Give me the courage to trust,
the capacity to dream,
the faith to pray,
and the generosity to love
when all I want to do is flee.
God, you called me forth to be your servant,
so now I pray.
Stand with me when I feel alone,
stand before me when I feel afraid, and
stand behind me when I want to turn back
from wherever you want me to go.
With you, I know I am safe,
for your hand guides all things,
calms my trembling, and uplifts my weary heart.
Stay with me, so that I may do your will
and serve you the best way that I can.
Amen.

Prayer for Discernment

God of direction and decision,
I do not know which way to turn.
The path is unclear, the way forward is confusing;
I cannot find my way. And so I pray, help me!
You formed the world and set creation in motion,
guided by your almighty hand.
In my wondering and wandering,
you are my guide, my star, my True North.
Help me. Show me the way,
point me where you want me to go, and
direct my heart, my feet, my course.
Lead me to the place I am meant to be
that I may fulfill your dream for me
and serve you as best I can, in whatever way I can.
Like those who first sought your Son,
I lift my eyes to the heavens, searching for a sign,
with faith, hope, and trust,
knowing you will never allow me to be lost.
Amen.

Prayer at Day's End

O God of the sunrise and sunset,
Thank you for another day.
Thank you for what I have been able to do today.
I pray it was all done in your name,
for your glory and for the good of your people.
As I reflect on this day, I recall your generosity and love
and wonder at your continuing creation.
Father of work and of rest,
Watch over those I love this night
and be close to those in need.
Remember all your children who have been forgotten this day:
the small, the wounded, the suffering, the poor.
Help me always to remember them and not neglect their care.
May they and all of us rest in your peace this night.
Amen.

A Prayer for the Pope

Dear Father,
Watch over and protect our Holy Father, the pope.
Give him strength to bear the burdens of his office,
patience to endure any hardships,
courage to make hard decisions,
and serenity to dwell always in your peace.
May he always approach your altar
with complete love, fidelity, and hope,
as a true model for deacons:
the "servant of the servants of God"
and a figure of steadfast humility.
May he lead your Church with tenderness, mercy, and joy,
radiating the love of Christ to an aching, broken world.
Finally, generous Father, be his consolation and his support;
keep him always close to your heart,
that the world may, in turn, be drawn closer to you.
Amen.

A Prayer for My Bishop

Dear Shepherd of all shepherds,
As you watch over your flock on earth
and over all who lead us,
I pray that you watch over my shepherd, my bishop.
Bless him with a sense of mission,
deepen his sense of charity,
strengthen his sense of duty,
and through it all, help him lead with gentle hands
and a loving heart.
Be his companion during times of loneliness,
and his counsel during times of decision.
Keep his heart joyful, that we may rejoice with him
and follow where he leads.
Help me to serve Bishop N. with loyalty and obedience,
with fraternity and dedication,
committed to his great work in my diocese
and your great work on earth—winning more souls to your Son,
and more souls committed to your loving Church.
Amen.

A Prayer for My Pastor

Lord,
Where do I begin?
The pews are not full enough,
our collections are not big enough,
the bills are too large,
the wiring is too old, and
the parking lot is too small.
And in the middle of it all,
there is my pastor.
Lord, please help him.
Help him to keep a joyful outlook,
an energetic spirit, and a forgiving heart.
Give him patience to endure many tests:
from the parish council,
the hospitality committee,
the altar servers,
the lectors,
the extraordinary ministers of Holy Communion,
and the people who don't like incense.
Help me to help him,
to support him,
to cheer him,
to encourage him,
to pray with him and for him,
and to be a sympathetic ear when no one else is around.
Help me to be patient with him, too,
for those times when he thinks

a deacon is more a hindrance than a help.
Help me to see him through your eyes:
as your beloved child,
seeking to do the impossible,
trying to save souls,
all while remembering that nothing is impossible with you.
Amen.

A Prayer for My Parish

Almighty God,
You created a home for your Son in Nazareth;
help all of us to create a home for him and for each other
in our local parish community.
Guide our hearts to welcome the stranger,
to feed the hungry,
to encourage the weary,
to clothe the poor and the naked,
and to see in all of them, and in each other, the face of Christ.
Send your Spirit to fill our hearts,
stir our imaginations, and inspire our souls.
Help us continue the work your Son began
in our friends and neighbors.
Keep me always vigilant and alert
to the needs, sufferings, hardships, and hopes of those I serve,
so I may serve them with fervor and faith.
Bless my parish with the gifts we need
to accomplish all you ask of us.
Give us wisdom, patience, fortitude, passion, and resolve,
and help us to love one another,
in spite of our frailties, our weaknesses, and our differences.
May we appreciate with every passing day this simple truth:
our obligation doesn't end on Sunday as we leave church
but continues every day, as we carry Christ into the world.
Amen.

A Prayer for My Marriage

Lord,
As I go about my ministry
and seek to live out this beautiful vocation,
may I always remember and cherish
my first vocation, marriage.
Let me never get so caught up in
schedules, classes, meetings, liturgies, and homilies
that I neglect my great collaborator in it all,
my wife.
Keep my heart always focused on
the vows I made to her
before I vowed my life to you in service to your Church,
so that I can be, first and foremost, a deacon to my wife.
Help me to remember to serve her before all others,
and to do so with tenderness and with passion,
with strength and with love.
Above all, with love.
Open my heart to realize that I am your deacon
because first I was her husband.
May we continue to grow together in faith, hope, and love,
so that we may serve each other while serving you,
as long as we both shall live.
Amen.

A Prayer for My Family

Lord,
Help me to be a deacon every moment of my life—
especially to my family.
How can I serve others if I cannot serve those I love
as a husband, father, brother, son?
As you watch over me, watch over them,
guide them,
shelter them,
strengthen them,
and enfold them in our Father's love.
Teach me daily to love as you love,
to be patient as you are patient,
to be merciful as you are merciful,
to be generous as you are generous.
Make me your instrument, Lord,
during times of sorrow and joy,
of hardship and good health,
of failure and success.
May I remember always that I am your child,
and that every day is a gift you have given me,
to spread your light in the world.
Amen.

Prayer of Praise

Lord, Mighty God,
who made the heavens and shaped the earth
and breathed life into dust to create humanity,
I am in awe.
Your majesty is beyond my understanding.
But today I praise you
for your generosity in the little things,
which your sainted daughter, Thérèse of Lisieux, so loved.
We sometimes feel so little ourselves,
but your love and your grace
continue to give life and hope and show us the way.
Here and now I praise you in the small things:
grains of sand, crumbs of bread, tears of joy,
a smile, a kiss, and the small hand of an infant,
clutching a finger to be reassured.
In their smallness, these things remind me of your greatness
and help me to be humbled by all you have given us.
Amen.

Prayer of Thanksgiving

Gracious Lord,
I thank you
for hands that hold,
toes that stretch, and
noses that crinkle when we laugh.
Thank you for the smell of old books,
the laughter of children,
and bells that call us to prayer
or awaken us to another day.
I thank you for soft grass and firm earth
and the thump of a loved one's heart against my chest.
Thank you for the gift of my vocation,
with all its challenge, exultation, frustration, and joy.
I am continually amazed at what I am able to do
with your grace and your love to power my days.
We fumbling, fallen, broken people
know that we are small
and that you are vast.
On behalf of everyone who might have forgotten to say this:
thank you for loving us anyway.
Amen.

II.

Prayers for Ministry

I once asked a newly ordained deacon what he loved the most about his ministry. He seemed momentarily stumped. And then he smiled. "You know," he said, "it's just beautiful. I can't believe I get to do what I get to do." I suspect most deacons would agree. We have the amazing privilege of being able to be a part of people's lives during some of the most beautiful, heartrending, challenging, prayerful, joyful, and agonizing times of their lives. What did we do to earn that privilege?

I still remember coming home from doing my first benediction. I got home around nine o'clock at night, and my wife had already gone to bed. I padded into our room and slipped under the covers, trying not to wake her, but she heard me anyway. She stirred and rolled over. "How'd it go?" she asked in the dark. "Great," I whispered. "I was wonderful. I didn't drop Jesus and nothing caught on fire." Long pause. She sniffed. Evidently, I'd brought home the unmistakable aroma of incense. "Greg," she said, "you smell like church."

That's the life of the deacon—and his wife. We may not always be holy, but holiness clings to us. These prayers anticipate and celebrate some of the wondrous moments of ministry that mark the life of a deacon. They seek to express the inexpressible—the deacon's prayerful approach to his ministry, often in times of uncertainty, when the only thing that is certain is that he needs God's help to serve the best way he possibly can.

Prayer before Serving the Poor

My Lord,
St. Teresa of Calcutta said you might come to us
in "the distressing disguise of the poor."
As I prepare to serve the poor today,
I prepare, as well, to serve you.
How can I do more for you?
What do you need me to do?
Help me to see in the eyes of those I serve,
in their faces, and in their outstretched hands,
not a neighbor, not a stranger, not a statistic,
but only you.
May I serve you by serving them
with devotion, with generosity,
and with love.
Give me this day the attributes I need:
patience, compassion, courage,
and grace—your amazing grace.
May I always see the God-given dignity of the poor:
those who are outcast, lost, troubled, and lonely.
May I always see in these people your beautiful children,
my brothers and sisters,
people of possibility,
people of hope.
Lord, as you hear the cries of the poor,
hear, as well, my cries for justice, for mercy, for security.
Show me how I can do my part to further your kingdom
here on earth.

Help me be your presence today
to those in need.
Amen.

Prayer before a Wake

Merciful and compassionate Lord,
The ones you love are grieving.
In this moment of pain and loss,
be with them and with me, your servant.
Give me the words to console, to comfort, to heal.
I may not know the particular ache of these people,
your beloved children,
but I know that you do.
Jesus wept at the death of Lazarus,
and you watched
as your Son gave his own life on the Cross.
You know grief.
You know sorrow.
Amid the complicated feelings
of loss, regret, anger, and despair,
help me to know your presence,
your love, and your grace.
May I remember the words of Christ:
"Blessed are they who mourn,
for they will be comforted."
May I share comfort and holy consolation
with those soon to gather to remember and celebrate
N. [*or* one who has died]
as we look with certain hope
toward the bright hope of the resurrection.
Amen.

Prayer before a Baptism

O God of all beginnings,
Guide my hands and my heart
as I help this young soul begin life as a Catholic Christian.
In this moment of wonder,
bring me to the banks of the Jordan
to feel the joy and astonishment
that John must have felt when he baptized your Son.
Bless what I am about to do through your holy will:
welcome a new member into the Christian community.
May my senses be awakened to wonder
as I feel the splash of water,
smell the sacred chrism,
see the light of Christ flame to life in the baptismal candle,
and hear the cry of a new life awakening.
May all these sensations renew my own Baptism
and bring me a rebirth of gratitude
for all you have given to me
and to all of those who call themselves your children.
Amen.

Prayer before Witnessing a Marriage

God of creation,
You created man and woman
to be companions to one another,
creators of life, and sustainers of hope,
through all the trials and joys of life.
As I prepare to witness this marriage,
help me to be your witness as well,
sharing in the power of this moment.
I thank you for this opportunity
to be a part of this celebration,
and ask you to bless all who will be a part of it,
that we might see in this couple
not just two people in love
but also you, expressing your covenanted love
through the sacrament of Matrimony.
As your Son was a guest at Cana,
be the unseen, but most welcome, guest at this celebration
and in all the moments of the couple's life together.
Amen.

Prayer before Preparing a Homily

Lord,
What do you want me to say?
What do you want your people to hear?
What do you want to tell them?
As I prepare my thoughts this day,
open my heart and my mind,
so that my lips might proclaim your Word,
your meaning, your message,
to a wounded and waiting world.
Amid so much heartache and hurt,
bring us hope.
Send your Holy Spirit to guide my writing
and focus my attention.
What do you want me to say, Lord?
Lead my thoughts where you want them to go,
so that those who hear what I will say
will hear not me but only you.
I am your pen and your paper.
Speak, Lord;
your servant is listening.
When you began to create the world, you said,
"Let there be light."
As I prepare to preach,
let me be your light,
to continue what you have begun,
and bring your eternal light to others.
Amen.

Prayer before Benediction

Dear God,
As I approach you in the tabernacle,
I pray to be made worthy of what I am about to do.
"Speak but the word and my soul will be healed."
Heal my sinner's heart, to love you more deeply;
strengthen my arms, to uplift you to the world;
sweeten my voice, to sing your divine praises,
not just now, but always.
I pray that I honor you at this moment
with simplicity and joy,
as an instrument of your grace,
so that all who bear witness to this sacred benediction
see only you.
May they be drawn closer to your embrace,
consoled and inspired by your real presence,
now and always.
I ask this through your Son,
who humbled himself to be bread
so that we might never hunger
and might one day gain eternal life.
Amen.

Prayer before Chanting the Exsultet

Father of wonder and miracles:
This is the night.
Tonight, your Church announces the scattering of darkness,
the hope of eternal dawn, the Resurrection of your Son!
As I prepare to stand before you and before your sons and daughters
to proclaim this Good News,
give me the grace to remember that I do not do it alone.
I stand in the company of angels.
I stand outside the empty tomb
with the women who saw and believed—
those first holy heralds of the Resurrection.
I stand tonight with all who have gone before me,
those deacons who have sung your praises
in grand cathedrals or humble huts,
in parishes and chapels,
and in temples made of stone or straw,
declaring to a waiting world: "This is the night!"
Father, you gave a voice to all of them,
who then gave voice to your loving mercy.
I ask tonight only this:
O God, who created me to serve,
help me serve your people this night.
Help me give voice to your enduring love.
Grant me courage to face the darkness
and joy to proclaim what your people yearn to hear:
that life conquers death,

that hope vanquishes despair,
that your Son has risen!
Heavenly Father, by your grace and mercy, we begin again.
This is the night when we remember how everything changed.
I give this moment to you in humble gratitude
for all you have given to me,
and for making all things possible.
Amen.

Prayer before Preaching

Lord,
Stand beside me as I proclaim your Word.
I pray that I will be your instrument
and you will be my voice.
Guide my thoughts and my tongue,
so that I may fulfill my holy calling
and preach your Good News with great joy.
I pray to St. Stephen, for courage;
to St. Francis, for humility;
to Mary, for obedience;
and to St. Joseph, for the gift of holy silence,
to know, Lord, when your word is enough
and mine is unnecessary.
Thank you for the grace of this moment.
Please keep me from screwing it up.
Amen.

Prayer before Teaching

Lord Jesus,
You taught your apostles how to pray
and shared with the world the Good News of salvation
with stories, parables, examples, and lessons,
using your own life and death as the greatest lesson of all.
Grace me with patience, wisdom, and insight,
to continue passing on the faith
that you have passed on to me and countless others.
Help me share my love for you and your Word
with those who are hungry to learn.
May I, in turn, learn from those I seek to teach,
bringing to this sacred work
what you brought to your own teaching—
light, gentleness, and joy.
Amen.

Prayer before Visiting the Sick

Divine Healer,
You made the lame walk and the blind see
and continue to heal wounded souls and broken hearts.
Accompany me as I visit the sick,
bringing only my humanity,
and the sharing of your tender love.
Make that, dear God, enough.
Help me to be present to those who feel absence,
to share with them a prayer, a word, a kindness, a hope.
May I remember that we are all in need of healing,
and that your grace is sufficient.
Strengthen my spirit, open my heart,
and help me to make you present today
to those I visit who are ailing.
Amen.

Prayer before Visiting One in Hospice Care

Gentle God of beginnings and endings,
Be with me as I walk with this child of yours
as her [his] earthly life draws close to its end.
May N. and all who love her [him] feel your presence,
your love, and your peace during this time of passing.
Lord, make of this moment a prayer,
that we may offer it to you
with thanksgiving,
grateful for the gift of time,
when time is so precious.
Help me to offer reassurance where there is doubt,
consolation where there is sorrow,
and compassion where there is pain,
so that I may witness to your goodness and mercy
and your tender promise of the life yet to come.
Amen.

Prayer before a Parish Meeting

Lord, God of unity,
We thank you for this opportunity to be together
united in faith as
members of the Body of Christ.
You know our yearnings and hopes,
our needs and our dreams.
Help us to make them yours.
Keep our hearts, minds, and ears open,
that we may serve each other
and our parish community.
We ask you to send your Spirit
to guide us, inspire us, challenge us, and uplift us,
so that together we may do your holy will
and glorify you with our lives.
Amen.

Prayer before RCIA Meetings

Father,
As we journey forward,
drawing ever closer to the Easter Vigil,
and the joy of your light in our lives,
I pray:
Help us to learn from one another,
to share with one another,
to be a source of encouragement and hope to one another.
Keep us attentive to your will
and conscious of your presence in our lives.
Bless us as we walk together:
enrich us, challenge us, sustain us, and strengthen us
in faith, hope, and love,
so that we may arrive at our blessed destination
celebrating the glory of Easter and the Resurrection
in complete and lasting joy.
Amen.

Prayer before Prison Ministry

My Lord,
You came to set captives free.
Help me and all who serve those in prison ministry,
so that those we meet, counsel, and teach
may know the boundless freedom of your love
and the consolation of your mercy.
Give me, good God, the graces I need
to proclaim your Good News
to those who are captive.
In the midst of my fears, give me courage;
surrounded by uncertainty, strengthen my faith;
facing walls and bars and fences, help me to see hope
and to be the compassionate face of Christ
to those imprisoned and in great need of your mercy
and your abiding love.
Amen.

Prayer for Police Chaplains

God of justice,
Watch over and protect those who watch over and protect us—
men and women who serve in law enforcement.
Stand with them and be their shield.
Help me in my ministry of service
to support and enrich their service,
with generosity, encouragement, fellowship, and prayer.
When the night is long
and the dangers unknown,
keep safe all who seek to uphold the common good.
Give their families confidence and hope,
to uplift them when they are worried
and console them when they are fearful.
May we always trust in you, wherever you lead,
and find our peace
in securing peace for others in your holy name.
Amen.

III.
Diaconal Prayers

Among deacons, there are three saints who are considered the greatest models of *diakonia*: St. Stephen, the first martyr; St. Lawrence, a great example of obedience and sacrifice; and St. Francis of Assisi, who abandoned himself to a life of humility and simplicity in service of the Gospel. In some ways, they reflect three aspects of diaconal ministry. St. Stephen, the preacher, was killed for what he preached (something every deacon should ponder before stepping up to the ambo!). St. Lawrence, when challenged by Roman authorities to turn over the treasures of the church, gathered together all the city's poor and sick, saying, "These are the treasures of the church"—and lost his life for it. And St. Francis, answering God's call to rebuild the Church, created a new religious order rooted in profound humility that sought to give dignity and hope to the poor.

These were men whose lives of service were radical, even courageous. What deacon would not want to have them on his side? These are figures who inspire, challenge, and humble us. They remind us what this vocation entails, offering examples of lives that were overwhelmingly Christ-like. Each saint, in his way, found a dramatic and startling way to confront a question that has almost become trivial now: "What would Jesus do?" The answers they offer should give all of us pause. May all of us find help and hope from Stephen, Lawrence, and Francis—guides for living in service to our Lord and to one another.

This chapter begins with prayers to these three great deacons. But the prayers that follow take us into other aspects of diaconal life, to circumstances and challenges that many of us face.

Prayer to St. Stephen

Feast Day, December 26

Brave St. Stephen,
You proclaimed your faith in Christ Jesus
to an angry and disbelieving world, yet you did not fear.
You gave your life for the truth you preached.
Guide my preaching and my witness.
Help me to have your courage,
your fidelity, your passion, and your zeal,
so that I may stand up
when I would rather back down,
and forgive those I would rather condemn.
Lead me to always seek Christ in all I do
and in all whom I meet,
so that, with you as my example,
I may one day see Christ face-to-face
and serve him for all eternity.
Amen.

Prayer to St. Lawrence

Feast Day, August 10

Kind St. Lawrence,
You cared for the material goods of the Church,
while showing great love for those cast aside—
those in poverty and those who were sick, suffering, or forgotten.
These, you reminded the world, are the true
treasures of the Church.
Guide my thoughts and prayers and actions
so that I may treasure those whom others discard
and be a servant to those in need.
Help me to see the dignity in every person I encounter—
to defend the defenseless,
give voice to the voiceless,
and seek justice for those treated unjustly.
Be with me as I seek to help the poor,
and inflame my heart with love for all God's children.
Amen.

Prayer to St. Francis

Feast Day, October 4

Good St. Francis,
You showed the world how to live with humility,
generosity, and joy—a true servant of the King!
As you modeled yourself on Christ,
teach me how to follow your example,
expressing tenderness and compassion to those in need,
offering fellowship and the Good News to the poor,
living as a visible expression of Christ's peace.
As you celebrated the world around us,
help me to also celebrate all of God's creation,
and see in it the wonder of the Lord's love,
making every moment and every encounter
a canticle of praise to the Almighty.
Amen.

Prayer for Diaconal Vocations

Lord,
You know the plans you have for all of us.
You call us to give, to love, to labor, and to serve.
But so often, we do not hear.
Father of sound and light, open my ears and my eyes,
so I may hear what you want and see what you plan.
Today, I pray especially for vocations—
that more of my brothers answer your call to the diaconate.
I pray they have the courage to say *yes*.
May those you are calling not only say *yes*
but also know the joy of embracing the call.
Bless the families and other loved ones
of those called to the diaconate.
May they trust always in your holy will.
I ask this through the intercession of your greatest disciple
and greatest servant,
the one whose *yes* made all things possible—
Mary, the Queen of Clergy, Queen of Deacons.
Amen.

Prayer for Priests

My Lord God,
I pray for my brother clergy,
the priests of your Church who also serve you,
and who have given their lives to you.
I pray for the priest beside me at your altar—
may he find strength when he grows weary,
comfort when he feels pain,
and consolation when he feels despair.
May he never lose sight
of the greatest gift of his vocation—joy.
Grant him the joy of walking with you,
who makes all things new;
the joy of Baptism; of the Eucharist;
of Reconciliation; of Marriage;
and the joy of offering the sacraments
wherever he can, however he can.
May he help witness your Gospel and spread your grace.
Help me to help him, and all priests,
as a friend, as a brother, as a fellow Christian
stumbling my way through life.
May I strive always to see them as you see them,
as imperfect men serving a perfect God
with fidelity and love,
seeking always to grow nearer to you.
Amen.

Prayer for Deacons and Priests Who Have Left Ministry

Gentle God,
Hold close those who are no longer serving
in ordained ministry.
You alone know their hearts.
You called them into service,
and now they are walking another path.
Guide them, that they may find the best way to serve you
and the human family you so love.
Help me, my brother deacons, and your priests
to remember their service and their sacrifice
so that we may continue to accompany these men
in prayer and in hope,
offering a supporting hand when needed,
and a shoulder when burdens become too heavy.
You know the plans you have for each of us;
may we always stand ready to live out those plans,
however we can, wherever we can,
with confidence, courage, and trust,
in whatever way of life we find ourselves.
We do this with abiding faith,
for we know that wherever we find ourselves,
you are never far.
Amen.

Prayer for Newly Ordained Deacons

Heavenly Father,
You who ordered the universe
have also ordained the universe.
You have ordained that the stars follow their course,
that the seasons follow your plan,
that the oceans and tides obey your rhythms.
And now you have ordained several men of my diocese
into your service as deacons.
Make of them instruments of your holy will.
Rinse away the useless clay, and leave behind new creations,
polished at your wheel, shaped by your fingers,
dried in the warmth of your gaze.
In the boundless mercy and love
with which you have formed them,
guide them with your Spirit,
so that they might complete the work you have begun.
Let them always remember
that they have been ordained to serve,
and not to be served,
to build up, not to tear down,
to preach, to teach, and to believe.
Help them to proclaim the Gospel
with the fervor of your greatest deacons:
as fearlessly as Stephen,
as compassionately as Lawrence,
and as joyfully as Francis of Assisi.
Make their lives models of Christ the servant,

that they may love others as he did
and always see him in those they meet,
even in the distressing disguise of the poor, the sick,
the lonely, or the lost.
Let their words be your Word;
their actions, your actions.
Make their hands your hands,
outstretched, to carry and comfort, to baptize and bless.
Grant these new deacons grace to be worthy of the work
they are now beginning,
so that they may one day worship you
in your holy sanctuary,
serving in eternal joy at the heavenly banquet.
I ask this through my Brother and Savior,
Christ the Lord.
Amen.

Prayer for Single Deacons

Father,
You have called people from all walks of life,
all stations in life,
from many places, beginnings and backgrounds.
That includes deacons.
I pray at this moment for deacons who are unmarried.
I know they can sometimes feel forgotten,
or even alone in a crowd.
Help me to do all I can so that they feel embraced,
included, celebrated, loved.
We are all part of one diaconal family;
help me to be the best brother I can be.
As we share the grace of this vocation,
and the joy and hope of our ministry,
may all of us—married or single—strive always
to fulfill your will for us in the world
as members of the Body of Christ,
each of us called to serve your people with love.
Amen.

Prayer for a Deacon Who Has Died

Father of mercies,
I pray at this hour for one of your servants,
a brother deacon who has completed his earthly journey
and entered eternal life.
Father, wipe away my tears,
and comfort all who love him.
Console all of us who grieve for him,
and as you welcome him home,
look lovingly on him with grateful remembrance.
Remember the times he prayed, sacrificed, and worshipped.
Remember the hours he gave to those in need—
those who are hungry, lost, living in poverty,
and those searching for your peace.
Remember the Rosaries he said, the novenas he whispered,
the children he baptized,
the couples he brought together in marriage,
the homes he blessed, the love he lived and preached,
and the Gospel he received, believed, taught, and practiced.
Remember N's family, who shared him with your Church,
and remind them of his love
and his continued presence in their lives.
Lord, I humbly pray:
May this brother of mine, this child of yours,
find peace in your presence and joy in the words
"Well done, good and faithful servant."
Amen.

IV.

Seasonal Prayers

The third chapter of Ecclesiastes famously reminds us, "There is an appointed time for everything, and a time for every affair under the heavens."

The changing of the seasons affords the deacon an opportunity to reflect anew on his ministry and on his particular role in God's ordering of the world. This is especially true of the liturgical seasons, which bring their own colors, customs, prayers, and rituals into the deacon's life.

At certain times—Holy Week leaps to mind—the deacon can be overwhelmed with duties, obligations, and demands. It can be stressful—for the deacon and his family. These occasions, I think, call the deacon to think more deeply about his role in the life of the Church and to approach his ministry with a particular sense of prayer and purpose because, at such busy times, it can be easy to feel like little more than a functionary in a dalmatic.

But these times and so many others are opportunities to remember what we so easily forget: serving as a deacon is more than doing; it is being. And that being begins, as everything should, with prayer.

Prayer during Advent

Dear Jesus,
The world is waiting—come!
As the days darken and the nights lengthen,
I turn to the skies and look for light
and plan for the moment of your birth.
Like your mother, I wait and watch.
Lord, help me to be more like her—
patient, thoughtful, and deliberate.
Help me, like Mary, to be ready for you.
When I become frenzied, bring me peace.
When I am too busy with planning, remind me to be still.
When I feel stressed, keep me calm.
When I am feeling the cold, warm my heart with hope.
In the excitement of this season, help me to remember
that the beauty of Advent is different
from the beauty of Christmas
and that Advent brings its own quiet glory.
As I light the candles of my wreath;
wear purple, the color of the twilight sky;
and serve at your altar with serenity and anticipation,
may I work to welcome you into the world,
most especially into my heart and mind and actions,
not only now but also in every season.
The world is waiting, Lord—come!
Amen.

Prayer on Christmas Day

O God of generosity and hope,
I give thanks this holy day
for the presence of your Son,
Emmanuel,
God with us!
I rejoice in the birth of our Savior,
the birth of renewal,
of justice, hope, and peace.
As your Church marks this day of days,
help me to continually announce his presence in the world.
Help me, also, to rediscover my role
in the great Christmas narrative.
Who is a deacon in this great story?
He is a shepherd, proclaiming this Good News to the world.
He is one of the magi, kneeling to offer a gift.
He is at times an innkeeper, too often refusing to give room
to the light of Christ seeking to enter the world.
Open my heart this Christmas and every day, Lord God,
to the beauty and grace of this miracle,
your Son, our Lord Jesus Christ.
This day, I who minister to your people pray:
Dear Lord, make me more than a bearer of presents;
make me instead a herald of your divine presence.
May I give you to every person I meet today and always.
Amen.

Prayer for the Christmas Season

Heavenly Father,
As I live these days of gratitude and grace,
celebrating the birth of your Son,
guide my heart, that I may mark this season as a time of joy
and a time of remembrance.
Help me to remember those who are too often forgotten
after the great feast of Christmas comes and goes.
Help me to remember the poor, who are still with us,
those who are sick, especially those without family or friends
to visit and care for them.
Help me remember those who are lonely
or brokenhearted, and those who are often left out.
Help me to remember the men, women, and children
living in the cold.
Lord, help me help all of these your children;
help me find ways to uplift them, console them, love them.
May I fight for justice for them in whatever ways I can.
When the music stops playing
and the carolers stop singing
and the world returns to what it was before,
may I continue to be a herald of Emmanuel
and sing of your glory, strong and clear,
reminding everyone I meet
of your greatest gift to our weary world—
your Son, Jesus the Christ.
Amen.

Prayer for Epiphany

O Lord of light,
Celebrating the wonder of your love
and the glory of your Incarnation,
I pray to remain in your light.
Keep my eyes fixed on what is above,
on the blazing light of your hope,
the light that guided the wise and the seeking to find you.
But also help me to see what is all around me:
those who, like the magi, are also seeking you.
Give me the patience and the love to walk with them
on their journeys and help them draw closer to you.
Finally, help me to look for those I too often miss—
those living on the margins, or hidden in the shadows,
the poor, the abandoned, the frightened, the hungry.
Help me to remember that so often
when I am seeking you,
it is through them that you are found.
Amen.

Prayer for Winter

Good and gracious God,
The world turns to you during this dark, cold time,
seeking comfort, warmth, and light.
This is a time when I often feel most alone,
most challenged, most uncertain.
I sometimes wonder if spring will ever come.
I turn to you now with my questions, my prayers.
In a time of snow, ice, and wind storms,
please, God, be my shelter.
And be shelter for this weary world.
Protect those I love and seek to serve.

Almighty God,
reassure me of your presence.
Be with those most in need—
the ones who need a place to stay, a piece of bread to eat,
a kind word, a welcoming smile.
Be the blanket, the glove, the roof, the meal.
And help me to be there too, as your deacon.
Lead me to be with those in need,
offering words of warmth and reassurance,
words of encouragement and hope,
words that bring at least some light,
so I can bring what you desire
and what so many in my world need.
Amen.

Prayer on Ash Wednesday

Almighty and merciful Father,
I pray this day as a prodigal,
beginning my long walk home.
As I mark the beginning of another Lent
and receive the mark upon my brow,
I resolve with your grace to make of these days
a time of prayer and penance, sacrifice and growth.
I am little more than dust—but I want to be more.
I pray to be more faithful, more forgiving, more patient.
I pray to be more by becoming less.
Help me to be less demanding, less selfish, and less proud.
Teach me to live these days desiring only to draw closer to you.
Yes, I am little more than dust—but I know
that you can help me be more—
more tender, more compassionate, more generous,
more of the disciple you made me to be,
more of the servant to others you call me to be.
Beginning this day, I resolve to give up
some of what I enjoy,
and to give more to others in need.
Yes, I am little more than dust.
I remember that what is now ashes
was once a blazing fire.
By your grace, reignite that fire within me
and keep me forever a child of your light.
Amen.

Prayer during Lent

Father,
During these days of giving up and giving,
I turn to you for encouragement.
I see my flaws and failings before me—
what I have done, what I have failed to do—
and ask you to bear with me, walk with me,
forgive me, and renew me.
Help me to remember that what I give up
matters less than what I give.
As I find myself consumed with plans and preparations,
for RCIA, for the parish,
for the coming liturgies of Holy Week,
this Lent, Lord, help me as a deacon to remember
not only how much I need to do
but also how much I need to give.
Show me ways to give of myself—my time,
my talent, my heart.
May I never hesitate to give food to those who hunger,
compassion to those who suffer,
attention to those who are abandoned,
friendship to those who are lonely.
Help me to see your Son in those who struggle,
fall, weep, and get back up.
This Lent and always, may I be ready to help them
face any hardship and carry any cross.
Amen.

Prayer on Easter Sunday

O God of the Resurrection,
I celebrate this day the joy of our redemption
and the miracle of new beginnings—
all by the grace of your beloved Son.
These last days for me have been a frenzy of feelings,
liturgies, prayers, chants, and deeply felt emotions.
I have walked to the table of the Lord's Supper
and followed into Gethsemane.
I have wept with Christ on the long road to Calvary.
I have lifted my voice in the last moments of darkness,
in prayerful exultation,
to announce this glorious news:
he is risen!
My heart is full of gratitude, O Lord,
and I search for words to express the inexpressible.
Here, all begins anew: life, triumph, hope.
I am weary and exhausted
from so much emotion and activity.
But I pray, once again, in thanksgiving
for sharing in this miracle—
a miracle of belief, of faith, of vocation.
Help me never to take this gift for granted
and always to want to share this Good News of our salvation
with a world so desperate to hear and welcome it.
Amen.

Prayer for the Easter Season

Almighty God,
In these days after Easter,
help me to see this season as a continual beginning:
a time when the world is reborn,
when hope is rekindled
and possibility once more fills the earth
through your Son, Jesus Christ.
With every "Alleluia," we acclaim
that death has been conquered
and we have been ransomed, renewed, reclaimed!
Father, lead me these days to a deepening love of my diaconate
and the Body of Christ you have called me to serve.
This is a season overflowing with sacraments and signs,
with First Communions and Confirmations,
Baptisms and Holy Matrimony.
May I greet these moments with thanksgiving and joy,
eager to serve however I can and to help welcome others
into the full richness of Christian life.
Amen.

Prayer on Pentecost

Father,
This day we celebrate the beginning of your Church
and its great mission that goes on throughout history.
I reaffirm here and now
that Pentecost was not just one day: it goes on.
By your grace and generous love, it goes on.
It goes on . . .
whenever acts of love are carried out in your name,
whenever the Good News is proclaimed,
whenever the poor are uplifted,
whenever the sick are cared for and the lonely are comforted.
Pentecost goes on.
Father of vocations,
I give you this day my vocation as a deacon
to continue your Pentecost.
Send down your Spirit, ignite my heart,
so that I may bring the fire of your love into the world.
Use me however you can, wherever you can,
to bear witness to your mighty works.
Help me to speak in a way all can understand—
and help me to do it not just with my words
but with my life—so that Pentecost lives in me
and lives on, as well, in others.
Amen.

Prayer at the Beginning of Summer

Dear Lord,
I begin this season of sun with gratitude, hope,
and a quiet sense of joy.
Help me to remember the source of that joy—
your generous love,
love that created the seasons
and continues to create delight.
As I mark a time of transition and relaxation,
when crops grow and gardens flourish,
I ask you to be with me
and those with whom I live and with whom I minister.
Be with us through long days and warm nights,
through times of rest and travel,
through adventures and misadventures,
through times as fleeting as fireflies.
Help me always to remember that in serving those I love
I also serve you, and my vocation doesn't take a vacation.
Open my eyes and my heart,
so I always see you in those around me,
through all seasons, at all times.
Amen.

Prayer for Late Summer

Dear Lord,
As this season passes and time moves on,
I thank you for all that has been—
this time of friendship and family,
of renewal and rest.
I marvel at your creation, in our world and in my life,
and I realize anew that this Ordinary Time is,
in truth, extraordinary.
Thank you for all of it—
the long days and starry nights, the smell of fresh-cut grass,
the laughter of children, the nearness of those we love,
reminding me of the nearness of you.
May I always cherish this life you have given me,
the vocation you have called me to live,
the sacrifices you have asked me to make.
All of it is a sign of your presence,
your grace, and your abiding love.
Amen.

Prayer for Autumn

Generous God,
We thank you, who have given us
the seasons to mark our days,
for the gift of autumn
and this time to give thanks and take stock.
As we harvest and plan for what comes next,
may I continually treasure all the good gifts
that make up my life and the lives of those around me,
especially the enduring gift of faith.
I thank you for the gift of my vocation,
the opportunities to serve,
to be present for you, who are present in your people.
Every Mass is a miracle, and my heart is full to overflowing,
just being there, inches from you.
Keep my heart forever alive in hope,
willing in service,
attentive to those around me,
so the seeds of faith that I have tried to sow
might reap a beautiful harvest.
Amen.

A Prayer for November

Lord of the harvest,
This is a time of remembrance.
I remember those saints who have gone before me,
known and unknown,
and all those souls who prayed
that they might one day see your face.
I pray for them this month,
praying with quiet hope
that I might one day be with them.
This is also a season of gratitude,
of reflection, and of hope.
I give thanks for the harvest,
for what has been planted, grown, and shared,
whether that is measured in produce or crops or lives.
With a humble heart, I look at all you have given me
and those I love,
including friendships, blessings, a vocation, a life,
and I am overwhelmed.
Lord, look with love on all who seek to serve you,
at the altar and in the world,
and bless us as we go about the task of living and loving,
in your name.
Amen.

V.

Prayers of Petition

We all have specific intentions we pray for at one time or another, asking God to intercede on our behalf for a particular purpose, problem, challenge, or struggle. They may be intentions of our own, or intentions for our family or community. How often have we heard someone say, "Deacon, please pray for me?" How often have we heard someone's troubles and quietly offered, "I'll pray for you"?

These brief encounters carry reassurance and hope that, really, is part of the power of prayer. The desire to be prayed for, or our willingness to pray for someone or something, lies in the heart of all believers. It is an act of generosity and faith. It forms a connection.

It is also a profound exercise in trust—trusting in one another, and trusting in Almighty God.

Prayer for Peace

Almighty God,
We your children have prayed for peace for so long.
I come to you again to plead:
Let there be peace.
Let it happen in my home, my job, my encounters
on the street and in the grocery store.
Help me to be not only an instrument of your peace
but also a champion of it.
I pray that I may do your will to bring it about.
I want to beat swords into plowshares—
help me to remember that some of the deadliest swords
are not made of steel but are forged with words.
Peace begins by disavowing name-calling,
bullying, and arguing,
whether it's while writing online or while standing in line—
in person or in cyberspace.
Help me as your deacon to be one who works always for peace
wherever it is needed:
in my parish, in my community, in my family, on social media.
Help me to live with the mind and heart
of your great deacon, Francis of Assisi,
to foster a spirit of sacrificial love within myself
and to be, in every sense, an instrument of your peace.
Amen.

Prayer for Those Who Are Hungry

Loving God,
Look with compassion on your children who hunger.
Be their comfort in time of need.
Fill them with not only bread
but also encouragement, consolation, and hope.
Remind them of their own unending dignity.
Father, help me to help them, however I can.
Place me where you need me to be,
to be the servant you need me to be.
Help me in some small way
to feed a hunger that goes beyond food,
that reaches beyond circumstances—
the hunger to know you.
Lord, give all of us what we need
to do your will for us in our time on earth,
so we may be fulfilled
for eternity with you in heaven.
Amen.

Prayer for the Homeless

O Lord,
You gave your creation its first home
and provided a shelter and a family for your Son
in Bethlehem, Nazareth, and Egypt.
Look with mercy on those who this day
have no home, no shelter, no family.
Help them find the sanctuary they seek.
Help all of us to work for a world
that gives them welcome, safety, and a future
for which to strive.
Protect those who are fleeing poverty,
persecution, or war.
Send them brothers and sisters to help keep them safe.
In my ministry, Father,
give me eyes that seek those who are lost,
arms that welcome those who are fearful,
and a heart that loves those who feel unloved.
Give me opportunities not only to serve
those in need but also to be their home, their shelter,
and their family,
by bringing you into their lives,
where they can dwell forever in peace.
Amen.

Prayers for Those Who Have Left the Church

Father,
My heart aches when I learn that
someone has left the Church.
Maybe they left in anger or in disappointment.
Maybe they found it too hard or too painful.
Maybe they left in despair.
The simple truth is that the brokenness
that fills our world also fills our Church.
We are a fallen people, seeking our way in a fallen world.
I pray for all those I know—
parishioners, neighbors, family members, friends,
people I used to see in the Communion line
or at Midnight Mass, who now are gone.
Our church is emptier without them.
I pray, too, for those I don't know,
but who are known to you.
May they find you wherever they are searching,
because I know you will find them
and you are waiting,
as a loving parent waits for a child to come home at night.
Touch the hearts of the seekers, the wanderers,
the worried, and the lost;
draw them to your heart.
It is your will that all may be one,
and so I pray that you help us all,
wherever we are on our journey,
to be one in you.
Amen.

Prayer for Hurting Families

Our Father,
Look with gentleness and mercy on families.
I pray for those who are wounded, suffering, broken.
I pray especially for families facing separation or divorce.
Help me in my ministry to be present for them
in this time of difficult transitions,
which is so often filled with crushing sorrow,
fear, and biting anger.
May I bear witness to your love and mercy
to those who so often feel unloved, forgotten, or alienated.
Lord, your love willed us into being.
May all of us who call you our Father remain in your love
and find a way to love others,
even when it is difficult
and the differences between us seem too vast.
Help me to listen, to give, and to forgive as I strive to witness
your loving presence within the community I serve.
Lord, help heal what is broken
and console all who struggle with separation and divorce
and all manner of family conflict and pain.
Hold close to your abundant love husbands and wives,
and especially the children.
We are all your children,
and we turn to you for a Father's embrace
and the love that never fails.
Amen.

Prayer for Understanding among People

Dear God,
You helped people of many backgrounds
understand your Word at Pentecost;
help us today to understand one another in our daily life.
In a time when we are separated by fear, bigotry, mistrust, and hate,
draw us together.
Give us the patience to bear with one another,
to listen to one another, respect one another,
and love one another,
despite the vast gulfs that seem to divide us.
Grant us mercy to forgive and to sow compassion,
wisdom to help us see beyond our differences,
gentleness to care more deeply for those around us,
and hope to desire a more perfect world,
the world that you intended for us,
built on peace, justice, and love for our neighbor.
Finally, grant me as your deacon
the goodwill and spirit of generosity
to be a bridge between people;
and by my words, my works, my witness,
may I help to unite those who are divided
and heal those who are broken.
Bless me with patience to see this world come to be,
so that it may be what you first imagined at the dawn of time.
Amen.

Prayer for the New Evangelization

Lord,
You call us to be evangelizers,
and you have called me to proclaim your Good News
as a deacon.
Inflame my heart with the love of your Gospel
and devotion to your people,
so that every gesture, every liturgy, every act of mine
may be an act of yours
and awaken more people to your redeeming message of hope.
Help me to live out this New Evangelization
at home, at work, in the wider world.
Give me the heart of a missionary, and send your Spirit
to guide my way, inspire, and accompany me,
so that I may believe, teach, and practice
all that you have commanded.
Lord God, make the great work of evangelization
forever new.
Amen.

Prayer for a Community in Crisis

Father,
I pray to you for the people I love,
my neighbors, family, friends, and parishioners,
as we confront this time of trial and testing.
We are feeling anxiety and doubt,
and we face a future we cannot possibly predict.
Father, help us to bear one another's burdens,
uplift one another's hearts,
and share one another's fears.
We know that your grace is sufficient,
your love is unending,
and the care you bring your flock will never cease.
Guide me as a deacon to serve those around me
and accompany those who feel lost,
so that together we may know more fully
the comfort of your abiding love.
Amen.

A Prayer for Life

Dear God,
Author of life,
I come before you to pray
for all those you have brought into being,
at every stage of life.
I pray for those smallest and most vulnerable: the unborn.
Protect them from destruction; shield them from harm.
Move the hearts of the world to bring the killing to an end.
I pray for the newly born.
How many times have I poured the waters of Baptism
over your little ones
and passed your grace on through my hands?
Be with them, now and always,
and walk with them on the journey of life.
I pray for those who face mental and physical challenges.
Their lives are a testament to courage and hope!
I pray for young people confronting pressures, anxieties, doubts;
reassure them, Lord, that they are loved.
I pray for couples embarking on marriage,
seeking to create new life,
and I hold in my heart those whose marriages I will witness.
Asking that I myself may be a witness to your mercy,
your patience, your love of life.
I pray for those who are sick and suffering,
especially those facing the end of life,
Give me the words they need to hear.
Help me, now and always, to preach the Gospel of Life,

standing up for the unborn and the born,
the marginalized and the abused,
the bullied and the broken,
the weak and the defenseless,
so that I may continue to serve those you have created,
with fidelity and with love.
Amen.

Prayer in a Time of Pandemic or Other Disaster

God of healing,
We turn to you in our time of need.
And we need so much!
Our restless hearts can only ask:
How long? Who? What? When?
And so we ask you to calm our fears and quiet our hearts.
May we learn to trust in your goodness
and your plan for our world.
We pray for healing and renewal.
Help us to grow from this struggle and sacrifice—
to grow in patience, in forbearance, in generosity.
Help me as a deacon to serve those in need
during this time of testing.
If I cannot be with them physically,
I lift up my voice for them in prayer and solidarity,
and I pray for the faith to see your hand in all things.
I pray for the lonely, the isolated, the depressed,
and those who do not know where to turn.
Lord, be their compass, their guide,
and lead them in love to your peace.
Gracious God, help all of us in the human family
during this time of crisis,
so that we may grow deeper in love for you,
and love for one another.
Help us discern with even greater clarity
your holy will for our lives.
Amen.

VI.
Devotional Prayers

Two of the most cherished devotions of the Church resonate in a deeply personal way for deacons: the Way of the Cross and the Rosary. The Way of the Cross binds us to the sufferings of Christ on his journey to Calvary. But it also affords deacons an opportunity to reflect on different aspects of our Lord's humility, sacrifice, and servanthood—qualities that are intrinsic to diaconal ministry.

The Rosary connects the faithful to our Blessed Mother, the Queen of the Clergy and the ultimate model of discipleship, obedience, and prayerful hope. I often tell deacons at convocations that Mary is a beautiful and challenging model for deacons. She is one who surrendered to God's will, who served faithfully, who journeyed where God led her, who remained with the Lord when others fled, and who uttered what may be the simplest, shortest, most perfect homily, in her final recorded words in scripture: "Do whatever he tells you."

It is my hope that these two traditional devotions—filtered through the eyes of a deacon and written with a diaconal heart—may help deacons find new meaning and resonance in these familiar prayers.

The Way of the Cross for Deacons

You see it often in parishes during the Fridays of Lent: individuals, usually alone, making the journey around the interior walls of the church, gazing up at the Stations of the Cross, to meditate, reflect, whisper a prayer, and move on. It's one of the oldest and most cherished devotions of the Catholic Church, but we shouldn't just do it during Lent. The Way of the Cross, really, is the way of us all—a way of living made up of struggles, burdens, injustices, and agonies. But we get up and move on. And we take consolation from knowing we don't walk this way alone. Jesus is with us.

In a particular way, I think, these fourteen steps of Jesus to the Cross can have special resonance for deacons. This way of sorrow and struggle, of perseverance and persistence, can speak to us and ask us to reflect on our lives of ministry and mission.

In his classic *Everyone's Way of the Cross*, Deacon Clarence Enzler concluded with words, spoken by Christ, that should echo in every deacon's heart:

> Seek me not in far-off places
> I am close at hand
> Your workbench, office, kitchen,
> These are altars

Where you offer love
And I am with you there.
Go now! Take up your cross.

Station 1: Jesus Is Condemned to Die

I adore you, O Christ, and I bless you.
Because by your holy cross you have
redeemed the world.

To most, he was just another common criminal, the kind who deserved the fate that awaited him. He looked awful: weak, filthy, bloody. If you saw him on the street, you'd go out of your way to avoid him.

And yet, this was the man who had mesmerized thousands with teachings and healings and miraculous signs that had transfixed all of Galilee. How could something like this have happened to someone like that?

The figure in the ragged robes, crowned with thorns, bleeding and in pain, helpless before the judgment of the state, is a reminder to us that the world is unjust, spiteful, callous, and cruel. This world will condemn the innocent, mock the righteous, and hate the good. It will break your heart. Given the chance, it will sentence the Source of all life to death.

Pause in silent reflection. Then pray:

> Jesus,
> I weep for the injustices
> committed against you,
> and against so many in our world.

I see you begin your walk to Calvary
and see the Savior of the world
humbled beyond recognition.
You told us you came not to be served,
but to serve,
and in this moment of surrender and obedience,
you serve all of humanity.

Lord, how often have I as a deacon
hungered for recognition, praise,
or privilege?
How often have I wanted people
to look up to me,
to consider me someone special?
How often have I forgotten
this moment of humiliation
and heartbreak,
when you showed what it truly means
to serve?

Jesus, teach me to give more
by claiming less,
and to live my life in service to the Father
and to those around me.
Amen.

Station 2: Jesus Takes Up His Cross

> *I adore you, O Christ, and I bless you.*
> *Because by your holy cross you have*
> *redeemed the world.*

How will he do it? How will this battered figure be able to carry that massive piece of wood all the way up that hill? He once worked as a carpenter, but he's spent the last few years roaming the hills, preaching. Will he even make it to the end? Perhaps the soldiers have a bet going: How long will he last?

The answer will probably surprise many in the crowd. He knows he has work to do, a place to go, a mission to fulfill. He knows they are watching him—not only the people there in the crowded streets of Jerusalem but also generations of people, billions not yet born. He is making this last walk for history and for the human race—for women washing clothes in Nigeria, for men planting corn in Nebraska, for children going to class in the Bronx, and for families gathered for dinner in Bangkok and Beirut. Jesus needs to make it all the way, to show how it is done and to live out what it means to "take up your cross." Ultimately, this journey is one not of defeat but of victory. And so he goes on.

Pause in silent reflection. Then pray:

Jesus,
How much weight can one person bear?
How far will you go?
The journey you are beginning
seems impossible,
and yet you do it anyway.
You accept what seems unacceptable–
literally, the weight of the world–
and take it on your shoulders for all of us.

Lord, there are days
when the weight of my world
seems too much:
ministry, work, family, parish life—
those times when the pressures are
too heavy, the obligations too many,
the responsibilities too numerous to count.
And there are times, too,
when those around me seem
to add more weight,
and the cross of daily life, with all its
challenges and stresses,
crushes my spirit.

Jesus, help me as a deacon
to carry whatever you need me to bear,
as a disciple, a husband, a father, and a friend,
and may I never forget that
you are always by my side.
Amen.

Station 3: Jesus Falls the First Time

*I adore you, O Christ, and I bless you.
Because by your holy cross you have
redeemed the world.*

Jesus stumbles, falls, and strikes the ground, and you hear the hard wood crash on the street. The crowd stirs. Could he not even make it the first few steps?

A pause. A breath. A groan. Then he scrambles to his feet. Once again, he picks up the beam and begins dragging it further, wood scraping on stone. He won't stop. Not yet.

A sob is heard, and some in the crowd turn to find a small woman straining to see but clearly worried of what she will find. She is instantly recognizable. It is his mother. The crowd parts, and she inches forward and catches sight of him as he staggers up the street. She closes her eyes and whispers a silent prayer, and no one knows what to say or do.

Some decide to move on, to see just how far he can make it. For years, he showed them the Way, and many followed. And now they follow still.

Pause in silent reflection. Then pray:

> Jesus,
> The road to Calvary takes so much
> out of you.

Yet you never pause, never stop,
never give up.
You do what is asked of you,
and then even more.
You walk, fall, get up, move on.
You show us the Way of the Cross—
and then the way of living.

Lord, some days I just want to give in
and give up.
I am overwhelmed and I make mistakes.
I try. I stumble. I fall.
I feel like a failure.
But my burdens, my crosses, are so small
when considered beside yours.
I realize as I follow you on your journey
that so much of life is not measured
in how we succeed,
but in how we get up when we fall.
Jesus, show me, a deacon of your Church,
how to keep walking,
even though the path is hard
and the burden is heavy,
and I sometimes stumble along the Way.
Amen.

Station 4: Jesus Meets His Mother

I adore you, O Christ, and I bless you.
Because by your holy cross you have
redeemed the world.

She looks as if she has seen a ghost, but it is her son. She sees him as she has never seen him before—bloodied and bruised beyond recognition, his haunted eyes fixed on the street ahead. He pauses, catches his breath, and before he begins to move on, he turns, and time stands still.

He catches a glimpse of her, and she sees him, and their eyes meet. It was all meant to come to this, wasn't it? He opens his mouth to speak. She shakes her head. No, don't try. A face appears behind her, and her son sees it is John, who reaches out a hand to touch her shoulder and tries to pull her back. She won't move. She can only look at Jesus, her lips trembling—or are they moving in prayer? Then the soldier blocks her view, shoves her son forward, and they have to keep moving.

She gave him life and now is witnessing his death. No mother should have to do this.

Pause in silent reflection. Then pray:

> Jesus,
> What went through your mind,
> as you saw your mother in that moment?

She was your first disciple,
and the most loyal.
She could not let you go to Calvary
without letting you see once more
the face that had welcomed an angel,
the face that had welcomed you
into the world,
the face that now looked
with unbearable sorrow
as your earthly life entered its last hours.

Lord, strengthen my faith
and steel my resolve,
that I may learn from Mary
how to live as your disciple
and always walk with you,
as you have always walked with me.
Help me, like Mary, to remain
forever faithful,
forever obedient,
forever trusting in your will for my life.
May I always see in Mary
a great model for diaconal life—
a life of sacrifice, service, and love.
And may my eyes, like hers,
always be fixed on you.
Amen.

Station 5: Simon Helps Jesus Carry His Cross

I adore you, O Christ, and I bless you.
Because by your holy cross you have
redeemed the world.

Who is that? Out of the crowd, the soldiers drag a stranger onto the street and order him to help Jesus carry his cross. Incredibly, he does it. The soldiers are degrading him, humiliating him, and he does what they tell him. This stranger picks the cross off the ground, and the scrape of wood against stone stops—and the crowd sees not one man being punished but two.

Who is that? Why would he consent to that? It's an astonishing sight: two men, one cross. Will they both have to die now?

But after a few moments, walking just a short distance, it's over, and the soldiers pull the stranger away. He stands there with dirt and splinters and sawdust on his hands, watching a criminal continue his march to death. The crowd looks at him and walks on, and all he can do is remain there, stunned and sore and filthy. And somehow changed.

An encounter with Jesus changes everyone and everything.

Pause in silent reflection. Then pray:

Jesus,
Did you think of the man they call Simon
after your moment with him was over?
Did you know him? Did he recognize you?
Did he realize what was happening?
You entered the lives of so many people
only briefly,
but changed them forever:
the blind, the sick, the broken.
Simon was just one more.
But his name lives on
in the hearts of all of us called
to help you, and others, carry the Cross.

Lord, if there are times
I feel some task is beneath me,
help me to remember
the humility of Simon—
the one who not only walked with you
but also helped you
to bear the weight of your Cross.
Simon served you in your moment of need
and is now bound to you forever in history.
Teach me, Lord, to look for
opportunities to serve
all who are burdened, overwhelmed, or weary.
Open my eyes and my heart to those
who pass by me on the street,
so that I can see not them but you.
Amen.

Station 6: Veronica Wipes the Face of Jesus

*I adore you, O Christ, and I bless you.
Because by your holy cross you have
redeemed the world.*

He hasn't really gone that far, but between the heat and the grime, the struggle and the abuse, he is unrecognizable. That face that so many know and cherish, that so many had wanted to touch, is dripping with sweat and blood now. The eyes that seemed to see into your soul, the smile—where are they now?

In his struggle he blinks back the sweat—or is it tears?—and he fumbles for a moment, trying to reach a hand up to wipe away the blood. Then out of nowhere, a woman appears. Is that his mother? No, it's someone else. She kneels before his stooped body, pulls the veil from her head, reaches up to wipe his face, and suddenly, everything is different. Yes. That face. You'd know him anywhere. That face. He looks into her eyes, his lips move, he says something, and she reaches up to clean his face again, but then a soldier shoves her away, and in a matter of seconds he is gone.

Yet he leaves his mark. She will not realize until later what he has given her.

Pause in silent reflection. Then pray:

Jesus,
In that moment, a lone person in the crowd
offers you the one thing you need:
relief,
to help you see,
to help you continue,
to help you do what you need to do.
This woman gives you
one moment of her life,
the one thing she could offer.

My Lord, do I give all that I can for you?
Do I strive to see you
when I see people in need?
Do I see you in all
who make their way to Calvary?
Help me see your face
in the weary, the hungry,
and all who are weak.
Teach me to use whatever I have to help
ease their pain,
so that, like you, they can see more clearly
the path they need to follow.
May I always walk with them,
kneel and pray for them,
so that in serving all those who suffer,
I will more faithfully serve you,
who suffered for the sake of us all.
Amen.

Station 7: Jesus Falls the Second Time

I adore you, O Christ, and I bless you.
Because by your holy cross you have
redeemed the world.

He has just rounded the corner after encountering the woman who tenderly wiped his face. Already the blood is beginning to stream into his eyes again. Maybe it's all becoming too much for him because, in a matter of seconds, he collapses again.

Where is the man who helped him earlier? He is nowhere. How about that woman with the veil? She is lost in the crowd. His mother—she must be there, somewhere, isn't she?—but maybe she just can't bear to look. There is no sign of her. He gasps, catches his breath, coughs. He is on his knees. He coughs spittle and blood onto the road. Then a soldier comes along and kicks him and screams at him. And Jesus can only look up. With a jolt, the soldier reaches down and pulls him to his feet.

Jesus stands up straight for one moment. For an instant, he's no longer hunched over. You can see his full measure—how he stood when he was by the sea, or on the mountaintop, or walking through Jericho, or speaking to the crowds that followed wherever he went. You see what he was.

And then he bends down to again take up his cross, and you see what he is: a man bearing the instrument of his death. He moves on. And you hear the sound again, the scrape of wood on stone.

He will not stay down. Maybe this is his final sermon, his last lesson: keep walking the Way, as hard as it is, as painful as it is. It is what we are called to do.

Pause in silent reflection. Then pray:

> Jesus,
> Your pain was unbearable,
> but you never gave up or gave in.
> You found the strength to go on
> and kept your mind and heart focused
> on where your Father wanted you to go.
>
> My Lord, there are days
> when so much of my life and ministry
> seem too heavy,
> too crowded, too difficult, too painful.
> I make mistakes. I stumble. I fall.
> I wish I were stronger, holier.
> As a man. As a husband. As a deacon.
> There are times
> when I am far from the saint
> some people think I am,
> and my weaknesses overwhelm me.
> Loving and merciful Jesus,
> give me what I need to get up and go on—
> a stronger heart, a wiser soul,
> a spirit of determination and hope,

so that I can live the plans
you have made for me
and live more fully as your disciple,
your brother, your deacon.
Amen.

Station 8: Jesus Meets the Women of Jerusalem

*I adore you, O Christ, and I bless you.
Because by your holy cross you have
redeemed the world.*

Some women had been following Jesus on his long, slow walk to the place where he would be crucified, and finally they couldn't take any more. He could be their son, a husband, a brother, a neighbor. He is a familiar figure in Jerusalem. Everyone knows him. They had seen him, heard him—wasn't he the one who healed that blind man? And now, this? How could this happen? How horrific are the thorns and the blood and the bruises. He hangs his head as he walks by, but for one fleeting moment he looks up, and one of the women sees that face; their eyes connect, and she just can't keep back the tears. She lets out a cry. The other women try to comfort her, but they find themselves overwhelmed. And then he speaks. That voice they knew so well is now hoarse, pained.

"Don't weep for me," he says. "Weep for yourselves. Weep for your children."

They want to stop him, they want to stop this, but they can't. They hold on to each other, and then the soldiers are there, pushing them away. And he is gone.

Pause in silent reflection. Then pray:

Jesus,
How many people on your walk
did you recognize?
How many in the crowd had encountered you
and been changed?
The lame, the blind, the sick, the lost.
Something you said, something you did,
changed everything,
and so they needed to be there,
needed to be with you,
needed to hope this would all end differently.
But what they saw instead broke their hearts.
Why did this have to happen?

My Lord, people come and go
in my ministry.
I see them in the pews, at the store,
at the soup kitchen, in RCIA meetings.
I don't know all their names,
but each one has a story, a history, a hope.
What do I give them?
What do I hold back?
In the daily grind of life, Lord Jesus,
help me to see opportunities
to give a good word,
a kind thought, a comforting prayer.
Teach me to stop and see in every one I meet
the only face that matters:
yours.
Amen.

Station 9: Jesus Falls the Third Time

I adore you, O Christ, and I bless you.
Because by your holy cross you have
redeemed the world.

For one heart-stopping moment, everyone thinks this is the end. Jesus fall a third time. and the wood of the cross crashes to the ground. But this time, it's different. He hits the stone street and lies there, motionless. Is he breathing? Is he dead?

But then he stirs. He takes a deep breath, gets up on one knee and then another, and stretches out his arm to try to grab the heavy beam. He wants to go on. He has to.

He stands, and a soldier lifts the beam onto his shoulder. He flinches, sinks, and it looks as if he's going to fall again. But he regains his balance. The crowd is quiet, wondering if he will actually keep going. Somewhere, a woman can be heard sobbing, "No, no, no!" Then there's the crack of a whip as another soldier barks at him to move, and some in the crowd start jeering, mocking him. But he keeps going.

Here is courage. Here is quiet strength. Here is a man determined to finish what he began for the sake of the world he came to serve.

Pause in silent reflection. Then pray:

Jesus,
I can't imagine what you must have felt:
the aches, the gashes,
the open wounds from the whips.
What you must have smelled:
the wood, your sweat,
the breath of the soldier.
What you must have thought:
"How much longer do I have to go on?"
"What will it feel like
to finally reach that place?"
"I want it all to end—but I know
there is even more."

My Savior, how often in my life I have
struggled and wanted to give up.
So many times in moments
of loneliness or doubt
I have wondered, "Should I quit?
Have I taken on too much?"
Life in ministry can bring stress,
worries, anxieties, fears.
I am pulled in so many directions,
with so many obligations,
deadlines, headaches, problems.
Am I even worthy to be doing
what I am doing?
But then I think of you.
And you are with me.

I am not alone.
Lord, walk with me on my journey,
so that I might walk with others.
Help me to carry my own crosses, so that
I might help others with theirs.
Be my arms, my shoulders, my legs,
so I may go where you want me to be.
Amen.

Station 10: Jesus Is Stripped of His Garments

I adore you, O Christ, and I bless you.
Because by your holy cross you have
redeemed the world.

How much more can Jesus take? He's finally reached the place where they will put him to death, and now there is one more indignity. The soldiers strip off his clothes. The bloody, sweaty robes, sticking to his bleeding skin, are pulled from him, and the crowd looks away. His flesh tears, the wounds bleed, and he looks like a skinned animal, already slaughtered. Some in the crowd start to leave. This is just too much.

But as the crowd thins, three figures remain: his mother, another woman, and his youngest follower, John. They hold each other, trembling. One of them is sobbing, but you can't tell which one—they are huddled together in sorrow, grief, fear. But his mother raises her head and looks at her son directly. Their eyes lock. This is the baby she swaddled, the little boy she taught to walk, the body she bathed so often at the home in Nazareth.

Love and devotion stand in quiet solidarity, even in his humiliation, in the last hours of his life.

Pause in silent reflection. Then pray:

Jesus,
You have stood with us in our humanity,
our shame, our pain,
sharing in our frailty and suffering.
And at this moment only a few continued
to stand with you.
So many couldn't bear it and fled—
inflicting the most painful wound of all.

Lord, you bore everything, and finally
stood stripped before the world,
showing all your wounds, your humanity,
your pain, revealing everything
we have done to you,
and you hid nothing.
You couldn't.
In this moment, we realize
what we have done to the body of Christ.
And your silence speaks volumes.
Jesus, how many times
have I added more wounds,
through my own failings, my sins, my
selfishness?
How have I caused hurt or hardship
to others with my words,
my actions, my pride?
How many times have I served my own
interests, instead of serving others?
Every time I see someone in pain,

bearing the wounds of life,
help me to remember
the wounds you bore for me,
and help me to see
not just another desperate person
but you, my Lord,
revealing yourself to me.
Amen.

Station 11: Jesus Is Nailed to the Cross

I adore you, O Christ, and I bless you.
Because by your holy cross you have
redeemed the world.

If there was ever a chance for things to change, for someone to offer a last-minute reprieve and let him go free, that moment has passed.

It all becomes finite in this moment. He lies on his back for the last time in his life, and they stretch his arms wide open. The crowd murmurs. The soldiers look restless, nervous. There's a shift, some people straining to get a better view of what is happening. And the relative quiet of the afternoon is shattered with a sudden, sharp BANG, as the first nail is hammered into his hand. Then the next. And then the feet. And then there is a discernible groan as the cross is raised and put into position, and he is there, for all to see.

You can't tell if his eyes are open, if he is conscious. But then he stirs. He strains against the nails and the wood, and winces in agony. It is clear the end is near. But not yet.

How much longer will it last?

Pause in silent reflection. Then pray:

Jesus,
You told us to take up our cross
and follow you.
Could we have imagined
that this is where it would lead?
Did we realize how hard it would be?
How painful? How brutal?
How much it would be
an act of self-sacrifice?
You preached love and mercy,
healing and hope,
and yet here you are,
a lamb led to slaughter
for the salvation of the world.

My Lord, if I ever doubted it,
if I ever questioned it,
if I ever took it for granted,
here it all becomes clear:
you gave everything for sinners like me.
At ordination,
I took your Gospel in my hand,
with the sacred commission
to "practice what you teach."
Now, I reflect on your sacrifice, your love,
your surrender during this agony,
and I wonder if I have truly practiced
what I teach.
Have I been worthy of this?

Have I practiced anything close
to the love you gave for me?
I know I have often fallen short.
Jesus, help me to grow in love and devotion
for you and your people.
Help me in my ministry
to open my arms as wide as you did
and extend my heart to those who suffer
and struggle,
especially those facing the agony
of injustice and cruelty,
just as you did.
Amen.

Station 12: Jesus Dies on the Cross

I adore you, O Christ, and I bless you.
Because by your holy cross you have
redeemed the world.

In one sense, it seems as if this day would never end. But at the same time, it has happened far too quickly.

In a matter of hours, he has gone from convicted to condemned to crucified, and now in these last draining moments, it is all drawing to a close. How is it possible? It seems as if it was just last week that he was walking along the shore, teaching on the hilltop, preaching in the synagogue, feeding multitudes, and making the blind see and the lame walk. And it has all come down to this?

The crowd has gone. The skies are dark. People know how this will go. They need to be home for the Sabbath. There are things to do, plans to make. A few tired souls stand under his cross. His mother is there. Her face is worn, her eyes swollen and red from weeping. She is spent, all cried out. All she can do is watch, wait, wonder. And pray.

He groans, and with a sudden cry, he struggles—and then surrenders.

The soldiers look up. His mother gazes one last time at his face, his open eyes still looking down at her, at us, at the parched earth where the cross was embedded in the ground.

It is finished.

Pause in silent reflection. Then pray:

> Jesus,
> In these last moments,
> What could possibly have gone
> through your mind?
> From the Cross, you saw the world
> you knew:
> Jerusalem,
> your family,
> your followers,
> and you knew what was about to unfold.
> The hearts that would be broken.
> The fear that would take root.
> The doubts that would spread.
> And the miracle that was waiting.
>
> My Lord and my God,
> here is your servanthood,
> stretched upon a piece of wood.
> If I ever wonder about my life,
> my vocation, my choices . . .
> If I ever question my purpose, or complain
> about the problems thrown in my path,
> I only need to look at you,
> giving everything here,
> for the sake of the world,
> to realize how meager my offering is.
> Jesus, help me to live my life

with humility, with generosity,
and with love.
Help me to take up my cross
and follow you.
Amen.

Station 13: Jesus Is Taken Down from the Cross

*I adore you, O Christ, and I bless you.
Because by your holy cross you have
redeemed the world.*

They manage to pull out the nails and toss them clattering to the ground, and then they take the body from the cross. His mother, pleading, stretches out her arms, her lips moving: "Give him to me." And so for one last time she takes him, and her son rests next to her wildly beating heart. She must be remembering all the times he did this, all those years ago, and the songs she sang, the prayers they practiced, and the plans they made when he was so young and could barely walk.

She gently takes the crown from his head, the device of torture that was woven from thorns, and her finger is pricked and bleeds. She winces, her blood mingles with his and collects on his brow, and then she pulls her hand away. She nods to the soldier, and her son's body is taken from her. John helps her up, and they begin to follow his body to its place of rest. Her robes are soaked. She is the color of crimson.

And then there is her face. For a flickering instant, you can see his face reflected in hers, and notice just how much the son looked like his mother. The resemblance is unmistakable—especially here and now, with her clothes, like his, stained with blood. From a distance, it looks as if Jesus is still walking through the streets of Jerusalem—as if his journey hasn't ended.

Pause in silent reflection. Then pray:

> Jesus,
> In these moments after your passion,
> the world had struggled to accept
> that you were gone.
> The earth trembled. The skies opened.
> And then there was your mother!
> She had to embrace you
> and then let you go,
> and witness so much suffering and misery.
> How can a mother's heart
> bear so much sorrow?
>
> My Lord, your agony has ended,
> but for many others it goes on.
> I think at this moment of others
> facing suffering and death,
> and those who will be left behind,
> to grieve, to mourn,
> to be overcome by the cruelty of life.
> Mothers and fathers, husbands and wives,
> brothers and sisters, and children.
> I see them at wakes and funerals:
> I hold their hand, embrace them,
> pray with them.

At the grave, I offer
words of consolation and hope.
But it is never enough.
Jesus, help me to remember
at these moments
what it was like for your mother,
your friends, your apostles.
Give me the words
and the tender compassion
to help those who grieve
for someone they love.
Amen.

Station 14: Jesus Is Laid in the Tomb

I adore you, O Christ, and I bless you.
Because by your holy cross you have
redeemed the world.

They took the time to clean and anoint his body and wrap it in white linen. There are faint markings on the linen—drops of blood still seeping through. That is to be expected. The pungent smell of the streets—the sweat and blood and filth—is gone. He is as clean as someone like this could be. The cramped space of the tomb smells surprisingly sweet. It doesn't smell like death. It smells like life. It reminds his mother of the vendors of Nazareth, selling spices and perfumes, fruits and oils. It seems a thousand years ago.

It should feel like an ending. But it doesn't. The quiet in the tomb is too immense, too still, too deep. If you gaze at the floor, you can notice splinters of rock lying on the ground. The tomb was recently completed, and the small shards of stone are still there. They haven't had time to sweep them up. But why should anyone care? It is done. In a few moments, the tomb will be sealed.

His followers are in hiding.

And history waits for the next chapter to be written.

Pause in silent reflection. Then pray:

Jesus,
As they laid you in the tomb,

many thought it was all over—
the story had ended.
In fact, it was only beginning.

My Lord,
Your passion reminds me that
the final word doesn't belong to death.
There is something more yet to come.
Your physical time on earth was limited,
but your presence here isn't.
You live on
in every continent, every hemisphere,
every home or hospital or school
that hangs a cross on the wall.
You live in the heart of every soul
who declares themselves a Christian
and wears a cross around their neck.
You live in tabernacles of churches,
in children being baptized,
in priests elevating bread
that has become your Body.
You live in deacons
who carry your Gospel in their hearts
and proclaim it to the world.
Jesus, your Way of the Cross is also a way
of living, of understanding, of learning.
May I always seek to live this Way,
so that others will also want to follow you.

For the Way of the Cross ultimately
is the way to salvation.
Amen.

A Deacon's Rosary: The Mysteries of Light

In April 2017, a a friend of mine in Michigan, T. J. Burdick, wrote a short reflection on the Rosary and the diaconate that was, in every sense, illuminating. He explored how "The Mysteries of Light," the Luminous Mysteries of the Rosary, make up what could be considered the "Rosary of the Deacon."

He wrote, "It would seem that since their introduction by St. Pope John Paul II in October of 2002, each and every bead prayed during the Luminous mysteries has inspired the vocation of a new Permanent Deacon. Diaconate vocations have risen significantly since 2002 and I have every reason to believe that it is because of the Luminous Mysteries."

What one discovers in praying and meditating on these mysteries is that they each have a profound connection to the diaconate. We come to appreciate how the ministry of the deacon is, in so many ways, not just a ministry of service and sacrifice. It is also a ministry of light. And it is a ministry with a beautiful connection to Mary—in many ways, the model of service and the model of the diaconate. Praying these mysteries from a diaconal point of view can lead us to think more deeply about Mary's role in a deacon's vocation and lead us to prayerfully consider how we as deacons can reflect her example to others.

May these mysteries guide us to a deeper understanding of this great work to which God has called us and lead us to prayerfully contemplate the beautiful gift of the diaconate—a gift not only to each of us but also to God's Church on earth. We are humbled to share this gift. Inspired by T. J. Burdick's insights, and with his unique frame of reference before me, I offer these reflections as a way to guide our praying of "A Deacon's Rosary."

The First Luminous Mystery: The Baptism of Jesus

This is where it begins. Before he will do anything else in his public ministry, Jesus comes before the great baptizer John, to present himself for baptism. As he did throughout his earthly life, Jesus "humbles himself to share in our humanity." And his Father expresses his profound love: "This is my beloved Son in whom I am well pleased."

All these centuries later, when the deacon baptizes, he repeats the ancient gesture of John. With words and water, the deacon is connected to this moment of light—becoming part of a great chain stretching back through the centuries, heirs of John the Baptist, heralds of life and grace and hope. It is the deacon's great privilege to celebrate this sacrament, building up the Body of Christ, using the living stones of the children of God as the bricks and the sacred chrism and water as the mortar.

+++

Good and gracious God, help me always to remember your Son's humility at this moment, and help me bring that humility to my ministry. May I always celebrate this sacrament with gratitude and joy—remembering that every child I baptize is your child, a brother or sister of Jesus Christ.

As John the Baptist did in the waters of the Jordan,
help me to be an instrument of your grace.
And so I pray . . .
Our Father . . .
Hail Mary . . . (repeat nine times)
Glory Be . . .

The Second Luminous Mystery: The Miracle at the Wedding Feast at Cana

Here, Jesus does something unexpected: he performs his first miracle. But it is a miracle rich with meaning, and it carries significance for every one of us. It is a miracle not of healing but of transformation: in turning water into wine, Christ makes the ordinary extraordinary. This is the story of every Christian: Jesus enters our lives and we are changed. We are water, and he makes us into wine.

The fact that this miracle happens at a wedding only adds to its meaning. Just as marriage becomes the setting, the starting point, for something wondrous and new, so too does this miracle during a marriage feast signal a change in human history, when Christ makes all things new. And it becomes, as well, the place where Christ's mother whispers her final words in all of scripture, her great message to the world: "Do whatever he tells you."

As the minister of the marriage rite, the deacon feels a close bond to this first miracle of Jesus and strives to serve as obediently as the servants of the feast, to follow both the words of Mary and the generous example of Jesus.

+++

Good and gracious God, when I witness weddings in my ministry, may I stand before the bride and groom as a witness to your love at work in the world. As the couple's lives are transformed, may I also be transformed—uplifted by your work in the world. May hearing each couple make their vows to each other inspire me to hear those vows as if for the first time, and may I hear anew the vows I have made in my own marriage.

Help me to remember Mary's words at Christ's first miracle—"Do whatever he tells you." May these words guide my ministry and give light and direction to my vocation.

As Mary was at the wedding at Cana, help me to be an instrument of your grace.

And so I pray...
Our Father...
Hail Mary... (repeat nine times)
Glory Be...

The Third Luminous Mystery: The Proclamation of the Kingdom of God

Jesus proclaims, "The kingdom of God is at hand." Again and again in his preaching, he reminds his followers what that means: a kingdom whose boundaries lie within the human heart. He calls the world to conversion, to a new way of living and a new way of loving. To those imprisoned by sin, he offers freedom; to those wounded by the past, he offers hope; to those blinded by pride or hardness of heart, he offers clarity and light. He proclaims Good News.

This is intrinsic to the life and ministry of the deacon. The deacon carries the Good News, the book of the Gospels, into the church, enthrones it on the altar, proclaims it from the ambo—and then lives it in the world. He is the herald of the Good News, a herald of the Gospel, a herald of hope. He gives voice to Christ's teachings and helps the words of Jesus come alive in all who hear them.

In his homilies, the deacon not only breaks open the scriptures; he seeks to break open the human heart, to fill it with understanding and call it, as Jesus did, to conversion. Proclaiming God's Word, the deacon today continues the great cry that Jesus uttered two thousand years ago: "The kingdom of God is at hand."

+++

Good and gracious God, when I proclaim your Good News, may I do it always with urgency and love. Enlighten my heart with love of your Word, and give me the words to make your message come alive in the hearts of all who hear it. Send forth your Spirit to renew me with every Gospel I proclaim, every homily I preach, every prayer I offer in your name. Endow me with the fervor of the first deacon and first martyr, Stephen, who courageously proclaimed your Word.

Like Stephen, help me to be an instrument of your grace.
And so I pray . . .
Our Father . . .
Hail Mary . . . (repeat nine times)
Glory Be . . .

The Fourth Luminous Mystery: The Transfiguration

Jesus takes three apostles to the top of a mountain, and there he is changed, transfigured before them. The light of Christ radiates throughout this event. Thomas Aquinas has called this moment "the greatest miracle of all," for it shows the perfection of life in heaven. It is also the moment when Jesus himself visibly connects heaven and earth, the divine and the human.

The deacon seeks to connect the divine and the human as well—bringing together two worlds, the secular and the sacred. He dwells with one foot in the sanctuary and the other on the sidewalk. At ordination, the deacon lies face down before God, literally laying down his life to be of service. He becomes at that moment a bridge between the people and God. He makes himself a living pathway from the valley to the mountaintop.

+++

Good and gracious God, help me to serve as your bridge to others. Give me the generosity of heart to serve my brothers and sisters with enthusiasm and selflessness, as I connect the two worlds of the secular and the sacred. May I never weary of doing your will—and may I also seek to live in your light.

Like the apostles who witnessed your luminous presence on the mountain, help me always to dwell in your light and be an instrument of your grace.
And so I pray . . .
Our Father . . .
Hail Mary . . . (repeat nine times)
Glory Be . . .

The Fifth Luminous Mystery: The Institution of the Eucharist

Gathered with those he loved at the Last Supper, Jesus left the world his greatest gift: his own Body and Blood. "Do this in memory of me," he said. To this day, at every altar around the world, we remember his sacrifice, his example, his undying lesson of love. And when we serve at the altar, we who are servants of God's people raise in our hands his precious Blood and remind the world every day why that blood was shed.

Serving at the altar, the deacon becomes a close collaborator in the greatest prayer, the greatest mystery, the greatest ongoing miracle of our faith. Like the apostles at the Last Supper, he is an eyewitness to God's transcendent love: love poured out into the chalice, love surrendered in a sliver of bread. The deacon assists in making Christ present in the world and works to carry that presence to others.

And the deacon challenges all to do exactly that at the end of every Mass: "Go," he tells the faithful. "Glorify the Lord with your life." Take what you have received, and who you have received, and make God known in the wider world by what you say and how you live. Do that in memory of him.

+++

Good and gracious God, may I serve at your altar with a spirit of true "Eucharist," true thanksgiving—thankful for the great gift of your Son's Body and Blood, thankful for the great privilege of standing at your altar, and thankful for the graces of my vocation as a deacon.

May I always see every Mass as my first, last, and only Mass. May I never tire of serving at your altars. When I raise in my hands the chalice containing the precious Blood shed by your Son, may I seek to use these same hands to uplift those who are hurting, those who are suffering, those who are hungry—hungry for food or consolation, hungry for shelter or justice or love.

In this, and in all I do, help me to be an instrument of your grace.
And so I pray . . .
Our Father . . .
Hail Mary . . . (repeat nine times)
Glory Be . . .

Prayer Intentions and Notes

Prayer Intentions and Notes

Prayer Intentions and Notes

Prayer Intentions and Notes

Greg Kandra serves as a deacon in the Diocese of Brooklyn and is a multimedia editor at the Catholic Near East Welfare Association. He is the author of *Daily Devotions for Advent 2018* and writes *The Deacon's Bench* blog. Kandra was a writer and producer for CBS News from 1982 to 2008 for programs including *CBS Evening News with Katie Couric, Sunday Morning, 60 Minutes II*, and *48 Hours*. He also served for four years as a writer and producer on the live finale of the hit reality show *Survivor*.

Kandra has received two Peabody Awards and two Emmy Awards, four Writers Guild of America Awards, three Catholic Press Association Awards, and a Christopher Award for his work. He also was named 2017 Clergy of the Year by the Catholic Guild of Our Lady of the Skies Chapel at JFK International Airport. He earned a bachelor's degree in English from the University of Maryland. Kandra cowrote the acclaimed CBS documentary *9/11*. He contributed to three books, including *Dan Rather's Deadlines and Datelines* and a homily series. His work has been published in *America, US Catholic, Busted Halo*, and *The Tablet*. He has been a regular guest on Catholic radio. Kandra is the author of four books.

Kandra lives with his wife, Siobhain, in the New York City area.

https://thedeaconsbench.com
Facebook: @TheDeaconsBench
Twitter: @DeaconGregK
Most Rev. Frank Caggiano is bishop of Bridgeport.

AVE
Ave Maria Press

Founded in 1865, Ave Maria Press, a ministry of the Congregation of Holy Cross, is a Catholic publishing company that serves the spiritual and formative needs of the Church and its schools, institutions, and ministers; Christian individuals and families; and others seeking spiritual nourishment.

For a complete listing of titles from

Ave Maria Press

Sorin Books

Forest of Peace

Christian Classics

visit www.avemariapress.com

AVE | Ave Maria Press
Notre Dame, IN
A Ministry of the United States Province of Holy Cross